GYMNASTICS
THE POMMEL HORSE AND THE RINGS

JOANNE MATTERN

The Rourke Corporation, Inc.
Vero Beach, Florida 32964

PROJECT EDITOR:
Genger Thorn is a professional member of USA and AAU gymnastics associations. She is USA safety certified and an associate member of the US Elite Coaches Association (USECA). Genger is currently a girls team coach and director at East Coast Gymnastics, Merritt Island, Florida.

PHOTO CREDITS:
All photos Tony Gray except pages 4, 11, 14 © Archive photos; page 7 © Reuters/Wolfgang Raitay/Archive Photos

DESIGNED BY: East Coast Studios, Merritt Island, Florida

EDITORIAL SERVICES:
Janice L. Smith for Penworthy Learning Systems

Library of Congress Cataloging-in-Publication Data

Mattern, Joanne, 1963-
   Gymnastics / by Joanne Mattern
     p. cm.
   Includes bibliographical references and indexes.
   Contents: [1] Training and fitness — [2] The pommel horse and the rings —
[3] The vault — [4] Balance beam and floor exercises — [5] Uneven parallel bars —
[6] Parallel bars and horizontal bar.
   ISBN 0-86593-571-8 (v.1). — ISBN 0-86593-568-8 (v. 2). — ISBN 0-86593-566-1
(v. 3). — ISBN 0-86593-567.X (v. 4). — ISBN 0-86593-569-6 (v. 5). — ISBN 0-86593-
570-X (v. 6)
   1. Gymnastics for children Juvenile literature. [1. Gymnastics.] I. Title
GV464.5.M38 1999
796.44—dc21
                                                    99-27924
                                                        CIP

Printed in the USA

TABLE OF CONTENTS

Performing a rings routine requires great strength.

CHAPTER ONE

ARMED AND READY

The pommel **horse** (HAWRS) and the rings are the most difficult and demanding of all gymnastics events. Both require tremendous upper body strength and intense concentration. Because of the upper body strength required, only men compete in the rings and pommel horse events.

Older and Stronger

When a man performs on the pommel horse, only his hands touch the horse. Sometimes they grip both **pommels** (PAHM ulz). At other times they hold just one. The gymnast also moves from one pommel to the other. At all times, his body must stay clear of the horse, and all his weight must be on his hands.

The pommel horse requires tremendous upper body strength, speed, flexibility, and timing. Years of practice are needed to master this event. It is so difficult that Peter Vidmar, who won a gold medal on the horse at the 1984 Olympics, calls the pommel horse "the monster."

Because of the tremendous strength required to perform on the pommel horse, many coaches think a young man should be in his mid-teens before he starts working on the **apparatus** (AP uh RAT uhs). Younger boys' bodies just aren't developed enough to compete in this event. So if you're thinking of beginning to work on the pommel horse, be sure to talk to your coach first.

★ DID YOU KNOW?

Staying Safe

Even a fall from a four-foot height can cause injury! Whenever you work on the rings or the pommel horse, be sure to place floor **mats** (MATS) around the equipment. You should always work with a **spotter** (SPAHT er) nearby to help you and catch you if you fall.

Gymnasts practice many years to make the Olympics.

A Pommel Horse Routine

A **routine** (roo TEEN) on the pommel horse usually lasts 30 to 40 seconds, although there is no limit on a routine's length. During a routine, the gymnast supports his full weight on his hands while he swings his legs over and under the horse without ever sitting on it. A gymnast's hands have to move very quickly, and his arms must be strong enough to hold his body away from the horse. Even the slightest bump against the horse can throw off the gymnast's timing and balance and ruin his routine.

Still Rings Versus Flying Rings

In the past, gymnasts competed in **flying-ring events** (FLI ing ring eh VENTS). During these events, the gymnast swung back and forth on the rings as if he were on a trapeze. But these dangerous events were dropped from competition during the 1960s.

Today, gymnasts compete in **still-ring events** (STIL ring eh VENTS). The gymnast has to hold the rings as still as possible while he performs his movements.

All ring exercises can be divided into two basic types, **hold positions** (HOLD puh ZISH unz) and **swinging movements** (SWING ing MOOV ments). Each hold position must be maintained for at least two seconds for a good score. Swings take the gymnast into a new position, which he then holds. Swinging movements must be performed smoothly, without shaking or swinging the rings excessively.

THE EQUIPMENT

The Horse

    The pommel horse is the same apparatus as the horse used in the vaulting event. The only difference is that two curved handles, called pommels, are used during the pommel horse event.

The horse's history is long and interesting. In the 1700s, European riders practiced stunts such as standing on their head in the saddle on a wooden horse. Once they had mastered these stunts on the wooden horse, they attempted them on a real horse. The original wooden horse was about five feet (152 cm) high and had legs, a head, and even a tail! Leather straps on the horse's back marked where a saddle would be on a real horse.

In the 1800s, a man named Friedrich Jahn trained on the wooden horse while in the German army. Later, Jahn became a gymnastics teacher. He invented several gymnastics events and was responsible for developing gymnastics as part of the European educational system. Because he did so much for the sport, Jahn is considered the father of modern gymnastics.

Since the start of the pommel horse, equipment and routines have been changed often.

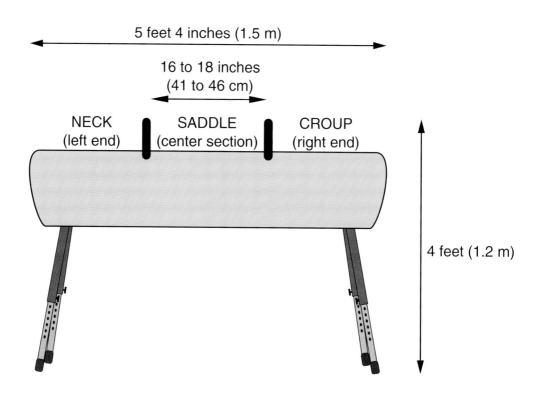

5 feet 4 inches (1.5 m)

16 to 18 inches
(41 to 46 cm)

NECK
(left end)

SADDLE
(center section)

CROUP
(right end)

4 feet (1.2 m)

14 inches (36 cm)

Jahn wanted his students to do some exercises on the horse. So, Jahn streamlined the horse and replaced the saddle straps with two pommels.

Today, horses are made from a combination of wood and steel. They stand on metal uprights attached to a heavy base to keep the horse steady. The top section is padded and covered with leather or a synthetic material. This section is about 64 inches (1.5 m) long and 14 inches (36 cm) wide. The distance from the top of the pommels to the floor is four feet (1.2 m).

Pommels divide the horse into three sections. These sections are called the **saddle** (SAD ul), or center; the **neck** (NEK), or left end; and the **croup** (KROOP), or right end. The gymnast must use all three sections of the horse during his routine. The pommels are about four and three-forths inches (12 cm) high and the spacing between them can be adjusted from 16 to 18 inches (41 to 46 cm).

The Rings

The rings were invented in the early 1800s by Francis Amore of Spain. Amore also invented the flying trapeze.

A rings routine usually lasts 30 to 50 seconds, although it can be longer. During his routine, the gymnast swings his body into a series of different positions, including at least two handstands. Each position must be held for two to three seconds.

The rings are the only gymnastics apparatus that moves. The rings swing back and forth as the gymnast performs his routine. Since the rings are supposed to remain still as the gymnast competes, he must use part of his strength to keep the rings from moving. This extra effort makes a rings routine unique among all gymnastics events.

Because of the upper-arm strength required when using the rings, only men compete in this event.

Many events require starting at a very young age to perfect a routine for competition.

Gymnasts used to compete on metal rings covered with leather to protect their hands. Today, rings are made of wood or fiberglass. During competition, the rings hang from a beam 18 feet (5.5 m) above the floor. The rings themselves are just over eight feet (2.5 m) from the floor and just over 19 inches (48 cm) apart. Each ring is attached to a leather or nylon strap that runs up to a steel cable connected to the beam.

Most gyms have a set of **competition rings** (kahm puh TISH un RINGZ) and a set of **practice rings** (PRAK tis RINGZ). Practice rings are about four to six feet (1.2 to 1.8 m) above the floor. Their lower height makes it safer for students to work on them.

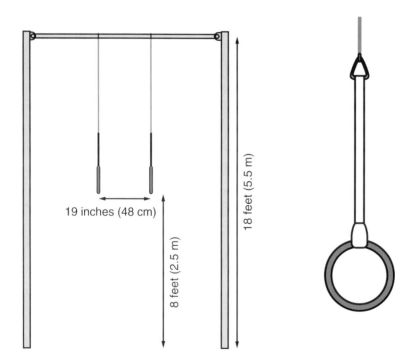

19 inches (48 cm)

8 feet (2.5 m)

18 feet (5.5 m)

GETTING STARTED WITH THE POMMEL HORSE

The two most important things to pay attention to as you practice on the horse are your arms and your balance. All the movements in your routine will be done with your arms in **support positions** (suh PAWRT puh ZISH unz). In these positions, all your weight is on your arms and hands.

To get the best support, concentrate on keeping your arms straight. Don't hunch your shoulders. Instead, relax them into a natural position. Imagining yourself being tall will help your body stay in the correct position.

It's also important that you grip the pommels tightly. Keep your fingers together and pointed in the same direction, and move your arms firmly and deliberately. Do not let your hand fly into the air or grab at the pommels.

The best way to keep your balance is to keep your center of gravity between your hands. When you swing onto one arm, don't let all your weight shift in that direction as well, or you're likely to fall to that side.

★ COACH'S CORNER

Which Leg?

When you perform leg swings to the right, swing your right leg higher and higher each time. When you swing to the left, move your left leg higher. Later you can try moving both legs together as you swing in one direction or the other.

You should grip the center of the pommels tightly.

A good way to build strength for a pommel horse routine is to work out on the parallel bars.

Helpful Exercises

Before you develop a routine on the pommel horse, you need to build up strength in your arms. You also need to learn how to shift your weight from one arm to the other. A good way to master these skills is to practice them on the **parallel bars** (PAIR uh LEL BAHRZ) as explained in this section.

"Walking" Exercise

1. Move forward and backward along the parallel bars using only your arms and hands. Hold your legs together with your toes pointed and your legs raised slightly in front to keep your balance.
2. Shift your weight from one arm to the other, making sure to keep your arms straight.
3. After you've mastered this exercise on the parallel bars, try it on the horse. "Walk" along the side of the horse by moving one hand at a time. Don't let your abdomen touch the horse, and keep your feet off the floor.

Body Swing

To perform a body swing:
1. Support yourself between the bars with your arms and legs straight.
2. Shift from one arm to the other by swinging your legs from side to side. As your weight shifts to one arm, lift the opposite hand from the bar. Remember to keep your center of gravity midway between your arms—don't move it from one arm to the other.

Leg Swing

Leg swings are performed on the horse.
1. Stand with your feet together and with your hands gripping the pommels.
2. Jump straight up, supporting yourself on both arms. Then swing your legs from side to side while you grip both pommels.

Mounts

Here are two basic **mounts** (MOUNTS) to get you onto the horse:

Front Support Mount

The front support mount is the same mount you use to perform the leg swing exercise.

1. Stand facing the horse with your feet together and your hands gripping the pommels.

2. Jump straight up and support yourself with both arms held straight.

Correct body position for the front support mount.

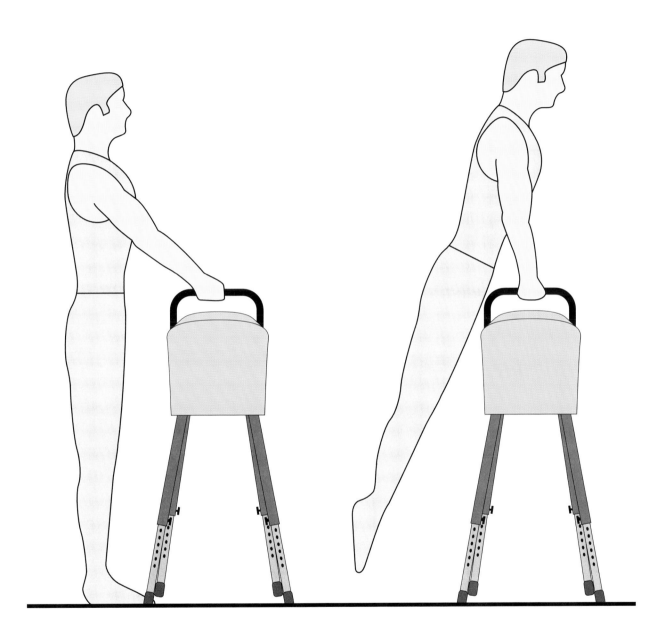

The front support mount

Half-Leg-Circle Mount

For the half-leg-circle mount:

1. Start at the right end of the horse. Keep your feet together and grip the right pommel with your left hand. Your right hand should be on the right end of the horse.
2. Jump up and straighten your left arm. Swing your hips and legs to the right, letting your right leg move high in the air. As the right leg rises, push off the horse with your right hand to gain momentum.
3. Rotate your right hip forward so that your right leg moves across the top of the horse.
4. **Straddle** (STRAD ul) the horse as you lower yourself toward it. One leg should be on one side of the horse and the other leg should be on the other side. Your right hand should grab the right end again. Your arms should support your body so that your seat does not touch the horse.

DID YOU KNOW?

Getting a Grip

Many gymnasts try to jump up and grab the rings. But this will just give you sore muscles, sore hands, and a bad grip! Instead, stand between practice rings that are hanging about shoulder height and get a firm, comfortable grip before you pull yourself up into the air.

TWISTING AND TURNING

Once you have mounted the pommel horse, it's time to learn some basic movements. This chapter describes a few you can try.

Single-Leg Half Circle

1. Start from the front-support position in the center of the horse. Shift your weight to the left and swing your hips and legs to the right. Your right leg should swing very high.

2. At the top of your swing, let go of the pommel with your right hand and rotate your hip forward. Let your right leg move across the horse and down toward the floor. The leg should pass between your raised right hand and the right pommel.

3. Grab the pommel again and stop with your legs straddling the center of the horse.

Single-Leg Full Circle

1. Begin a single-leg full circle by performing a single-leg half circle.

2. As you come down into the straddle position, let your right leg continue its swing and move toward the left end of the horse.

3. Release the left pommel so that your right leg passes through the space between your left hand and the pommel.

4. Grab the pommel again as soon as your leg has passed through. You should end in the front-support position.

A young gymnast demonstrates the single-leg half circle on the pommel horse. Notice how rigid the body remains.

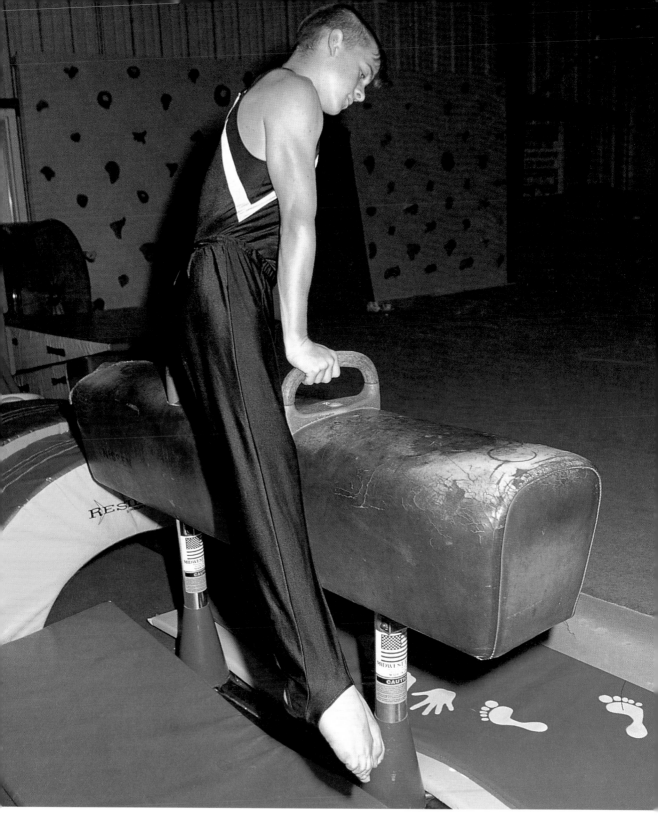

Body momentum is important to perform a double-leg circle.

Double-Leg Circles
1. Start in the front mount support position.
2. Rock your weight left, then right to gain momentum.
Keep a tight grip on the pommels.
3. As you gain speed, send your legs over the horse in
either direction. As you do this you must lift your hand off
the pommel to allow your legs to pass through.
4. Continue on around the horse remembering to lift each
hand as your legs pass.

You will find that your speed will carry you around the
horse in a circle. Keep your body tight and straight.

Getting Off the Horse
There are several ways to get off, or **dismount** (DISS
MOUNT) from, the horse. No matter which dismount you
use, you should always land on the balls of your feet, with
your knees bent to absorb the impact. One hand should be
on the horse, while the other is stretched up or to the side.
As soon as you land, drop down onto your heels,
straighten your legs, move your hands to your sides, and
stand at attention.

Single Rear Dismount

   The single rear dismount is a basic dismount.

1. Begin with a right **feint** (FAYNT), as you swing your right leg over the horse.

2. Once the right leg reaches the rear of the horse, bring it alongside your left leg. Swing both legs forward so they are high in the air and moving across the left end of the horse.

3. Let go of the left pommel. Your legs should move through the open space and down to the floor.

4. As you land, extend your right arm to the side. Your left hand should be holding the left pommel.

A single rear dismount should start with a feint to enable the gymnast to gain speed.

Remember to land with your knees slightly bent to absorb the shock.

Feints

Feints are circular movements in which the hands do not leave the pommels. Feints are a great way to build momentum for a dismount or for an advanced stunt. A feint can be made either to the right or to the left. Just one leg can move, or both legs can move together.

To perform a right feint, shift your weight onto your right arm and swing your right leg across the horse. Remember not to let go of the pommels! You should end with your legs straddling your right arm. To perform a left feint, follow the same procedure using your left hand and leg.

★ DID YOU KNOW?

Right and Left

It's a good idea to practice the single rear dismount from a right feint and a left feint position. That way, you have two separate dismounts instead of just one!

CHAPTER FIVE

SWINGS AND HANGS

Getting Ready for the Rings

Chin-ups are the best exercise to prepare you for ring work. Hold the rings in a comfortable grip, with your fingers pointed toward you. Then use your shoulders to pull yourself straight up.

Later, when your arms and shoulders have gained strength, try starting the chin-up from a hanging position. Grip the rings and bend your legs so you are kneeling in mid-air. Then pull yourself straight up. Your legs should straighten at the top of the chin-up and return to a bent position as you lower yourself.

Mounts

No fancy moves are used to mount the rings. Some gymnasts simply jump up and grab the rings. However, this movement causes the rings to move, and the gymnast has to wait until they are still to start his routine.

A better way to mount is to have a teammate or your coach stand behind you and lift you up to the rings. When you have a secure grip, let your partner know and he will release you so you can start your routine.

Swings

A swing is a back-and-forth movement from a hanging position.

Pendulum Swing

All ring routines begin with the gymnast in a motionless position on the rings. The pendulum swing is an excellent way to gain enough momentum to move into your routine.

1. As you hang from the rings, begin by bending your waist and raising your legs forward. Be sure to hold them as straight as you can.
2. When your legs are parallel to the floor, let them drop down and back until your body is **arched** (AHRCHT).
3. Swing your legs up and forward again. Meanwhile, bend slightly at the waist and pull up on your arms so that your body is raised toward the rings at the top of your forward swing.
4. Repeat steps two and three until you've gained enough momentum to continue with your next movement.

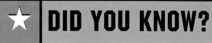

★ DID YOU KNOW?

Keep Still!
Remember that the rings should stay as motionless as possible as you perform a pendulum swing, or any other movement. Think about your body and make your movements as controlled as possible.

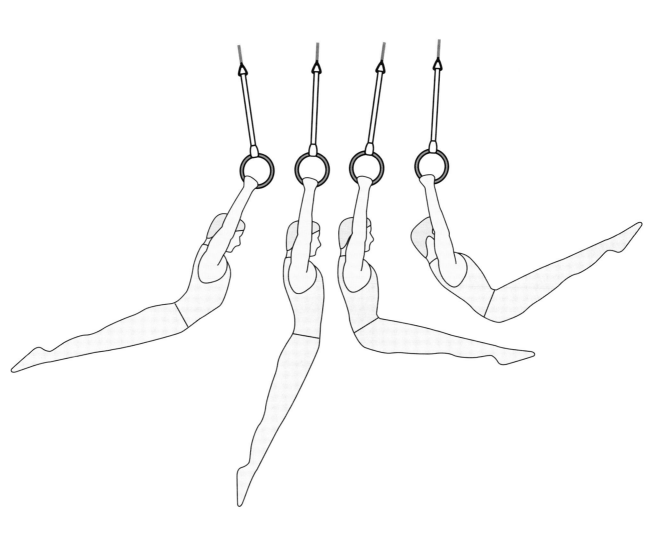

The pendulum swing

The body should be in this position at the final step of skin-the-cat.

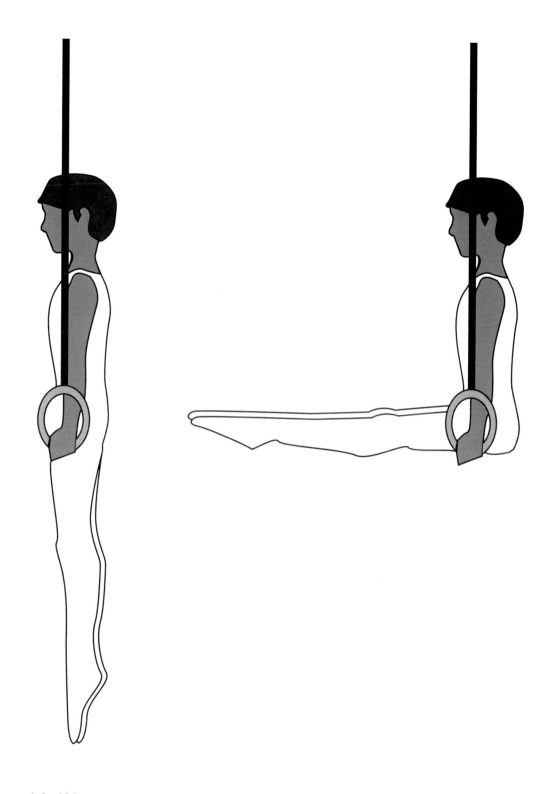

A half-lever

Bent Body Inverted Hang

1. Using the pendulum swing, let your legs travel up and between the ring straps.

2. Straighten your legs so that they are parallel to the floor and above your face. Your eyes should be looking directly at your knees.

3. Remain in the hold position for several counts. Then reverse the process to return to your starting position. Be sure to keep your legs straight at all times!

Hanging Half Lever

   To do a hanging half lever:

1. Start with a pendulum swing.

2. Stop and hold your legs straight out in front of you, as if you were sitting down. Keep your back and legs straight.

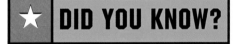

★ DID YOU KNOW?

Keep Your Head!

   To perform the single-leg cutoff correctly, your head must be held forward with your chin almost on your chest. Keep your eyes on the ring so you can catch it as soon as your leg passes it.

Dismounts

A strong dismount will give a dramatic finish to your routine. Even a simple dismount can look exciting!

Backward-Straddle Dismount

1. As your body swings into a hanging position, straighten your legs. Then pump them backward to gain momentum.
2. Swing forward and move your body into a **pike** (PIK) position with your legs straight up in the air.
3. As your legs move up, move them to the outside of the rings and into a straddle position.
4. As your legs pass the straps, lift your body and throw back your head.
5. Release the rings as your legs travel in an arc over your head. Then let your legs drop to the floor for the landing.

★ **DID YOU KNOW?**

Safety Belts

Performing on the rings can be dangerous, especially when the gymnast is upside-down! Many gymnasts use **safety belts** (SAYF tee BELTS) when they are learning a new move on the rings. The gymnast wears a belt around his waist. The belt is connected to ropes hanging from the ceiling or held by spotters. If the gymnast starts to fall, the ropes will hold him above the floor and prevent serious injury.

Flyaway Dismount

1. Swing your legs forward and up so that your feet pass between the rings.

2. As your feet pass between the rings, extend your body so that you swing down and out.

3. Let go of the rings and fly forward to land on the balls of your feet.

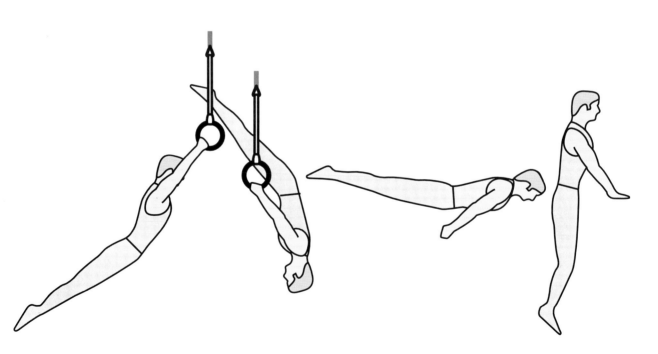

A flyaway dismount

To have a perfect landing, remain balanced and in control when your feet touch the ground.

Landing

You should always land on the balls of your feet with your legs close together. Both feet should hit the mat at the same time. Bend your knees to absorb the impact, and keep your body slightly forward for balance. Hold your arms in any position that is comfortable, such as over your head or out to the sides. Come to attention—legs straight, hands at your sides—as soon as you hit the floor.

 **DID YOU KNOW?**

Practice Each Part

To learn any dismount, it's best to practice each part of it separately. For example, when you are learning the backward-straddle dismount, practice swinging your legs up and into the pike position. Then practice lifting your body and throwing your head back. Once you've mastered each part of the dismount, you're ready to try the whole movement from start to finish.

GLOSSARY

apparatus (AP uh RAT uhs) — a special piece of equipment for performing a gymnastic event

arch (AHRCH) — a position in which the upper and lower parts of your body form a slight curve

competition rings (kahm puh TISH un RINGZ) — rings that are set at competition height, just over eight feet (2.5 m) above the floor

croup (KROOP) — the right end of the horse

dismount (DISS MOUNT) — to get off an apparatus

feint (FAYNT) — a circular movement in which the hands do not leave the pommels

flying-ring event (FLI ing ring eh VENT) — a routine in which the gymnast swings back and forth on the rings

hold position (HOLD puh ZISH un) — a position in which the gymnast holds his body motionless for at least two seconds

horse (HAWRS) — a piece of gymnastics equipment used in vaulting and pommel horse events

mat (MAT) — a padded surface that provides a soft, safe landing place for a gymnast

mount (MOUNT) — to get on an apparatus

neck (NEK) — the left end of the horse

parallel bars (PAIR uh LEL BAHRZ) — a gymnastic apparatus made up of two bars running side by side and standing just over five and one-half feet (1.5 m) high

GLOSSARY

pike (PIK) — a position in which the legs are straight and the body is folded at the waist

pommel (PAHM ul) — the curved handles on top of a horse

practice rings (PRAK tis RINGZ) — rings that are set four to six feet (1.2 to 1.8 m) above the floor

routine (roo TEEN) — a combination of moves displaying a full range of skills

saddle (SAD ul) — the center part of the horse

safety belt (SAYF tee BELT) — a belt or harness worn by a gymnast to prevent falls

spotter (SPAHT er) — a coach or experienced gymnast who stands below a gymnast to give advice and catch him or her in the event of a fall

still-ring event (STIL ring eh VENT) — a routine in which the gymnast holds the rings as still as possible as he performs his routine

straddle (STRAD ul) — a position in which the legs are held straight and apart across an apparatus

support position (suh PAWRT puh ZISH un) — a position where the body is supported on the arms and hands

swinging movements (SWING ing MOOV ments) — movements in which the gymnast moves through the air while gripping the rings

travel (TRAV ul) — a movement that carries a gymnast from one part of the horse to another

FURTHER READING

Find out more about the pommel horse and the rings from these helpful books, magazines, and information sites:

- Feeney, Rik. *Gymnastics: A Guide for Parents and Athletes.* Indianapolis: Masters Press, 1992.
- Gutman, Dan. *Gymnastics.* New York: Viking, 1996.
- Marks, Marjorie. *A Basic Guide to Gymnastics: An Official U.S. Olympic Committee Sports Series.* Glendale, CA: Griffin Publishing, 1998.
- Peszek, Luan. *The Gymnastics Almanac.* Los Angeles: Lowell House, 1998.
- *USA Gymnastics Safety Handbook.* Indianapolis: USA Gymnastics, 1998.

- *USA Gymnastics*—This magazines covers American competitions and athletes, as well as major competitions leading up to the Olympics.
- *Technique*—This publication is geared toward coaches and judges.
- *International Gymnast*—This magazine covers both American and international competitions and athletes.

- www.usa-gymnastics.org
  This is the official Website of USA Gymnastics, the national governing body for gymnastics in the United States.
- www.ngja.org
  National Gymnastics Judges Association, Inc.
- www.ngja.org
  This is the official Website for the National Gymnastics Judges Association, Inc.

INDEX

DATE DUE
